Th

Florian Zeller is a French pl
L'Autre, *Le Manège*, *Si tu mourais*, *_*
(*The Truth*), *La Mère* (*The Mother*) and *Le Père* (*The Father*),
which has been produced in more than fifty countries and has
won many awards worldwide. *The Father*, directed by Florian
Zeller, was adapted for the screen with Christopher Hampton,
won numerous awards, including both an Oscar and BAFTA
for Best Adapted Screenplay, and an Oscar and BAFTA for
Best Actor (Anthony Hopkins). *Une Heure de tranquillité* (*A
Bit of Peace and Quiet*) opened with Fabrice Luchini, and has
since been adapted for the screen, directed by Patrice Leconte.
Le Mensonge (*The Lie*) was staged in 2015 and *L'Envers du
décor* opened in January 2016 at the Théâtre de Paris, starring
Daniel Auteuil, and *Avant de s'envoler* (*The Height of the
Storm*) at the Théâtre de l'Oeuvre in October 2016. *The Son*,
completing his 'Family Trilogy', was produced in Paris in 2018
before its London premiere at the Kiln Theatre in 2019. It was
revived at the Duke of York's Theatre later that year. It was
adapted for the screen in 2021, directed by Florian Zeller.

Christopher Hampton was born in the Azores in 1946. He
wrote his first play, *When Did You Last See My Mother?*, at
the age of eighteen. Since then, his plays have included *The
Philanthropist*, *Savages*, *Tales from Hollywood*, *Les Liaisons
Dangereuses*, *White Chameleon*, *The Talking Cure*,
Appomattox and *A German Life*. He has translated plays by
Ibsen, Molière, von Horváth, Chekhov and Yasmina Reza. This
is his seventh translation of a play by Florian Zeller, including
The Father, which he subsequently co-wrote for the screen
with Florian Zeller. His television work includes adaptations of
The History Man, *Hôtel du Lac* and *The Singapore Grip*. His
screenplays include *The Honorary Consul*, *The Good Father*,
Dangerous Liaisons, *Mary Reilly*, *Total Eclipse*, *The Quiet
American*, *Atonement*, *Cheri*, *A Dangerous Method*,
Carrington, *The Secret Agent* and *Imagining Argentina*, the
last three of which he also directed.

FLORIAN ZELLER

The Forest

translated by
CHRISTOPHER HAMPTON

faber

First published in 2022
by Faber and Faber Limited
74–77 Great Russell Street, London WC1B 3DA

Typeset by Brighton Gray
Printed and bound in the UK by CPI Group (Ltd), Croydon CR0 4YY

A CIP record for this book
is available from the British Library

ISBN 978–0–571–37692–6

2 4 6 8 10 9 7 5 3 1

The Forest in this translation by Christopher Hampton
was first performed at the Hampstead Theatre, London,
on 5 February 2022. The cast, in order of appearance, was
as follows:

Man 1 Toby Stephens
Wife Gina McKee
Daughter Millie Brady
Man 2 Paul McGann
Girlfriend Angel Coulby
Young Man Eddie Toll
Male Friend Silas Carson
Female Friend Sakuntala Ramanee
Man in Black Finbar Lynch

Director Jonathan Kent
Designer Anna Fleischle
Lighting Hugh Vanstone
Sound Isobel Waller-Bridge
Casting Lotte Hines

Characters

Man 1

Wife

Daughter

Man 2

Girlfriend

Young Man

Male Friend

Female Friend

Man in Black
who wears a particular kind of whitened make-up, which
makes him look as if he's emerged from a nightmare

Setting

Set 1 (S1): a living room
Set 2 (S2): a bedroom
Set 3 (S3): an office

*These three sets need to coexist on the same stage. They can
be lit, or in darkness, alternately, so that to start with the
three different areas appear to be completely
compartmentalised. However, as the play proceeds,
impressions of overflow, interpenetration, indeed
simultaneity may begin to be experienced.*

THE FOREST

Act One

ONE

(*S1*): *Man 1, his Wife, his Daughter.*

Wife Ah, there you are.

Man 1 Yes. I've only just finished.

He takes off his coat. He kisses his wife.

Wife Did you get my message?

Man 1 Yes, of course. Is she still here?

Wife She's in the kitchen.

Man 1 Is she all right?

Wife She's been crying all evening.

Man 1 Poor little thing.

Wife Yes. She was bound to end up the victim.

Man 1 And I'm supposed to know about this? I mean . . .

Wife Yes. I told her I'd told you.

Man 1 Good. I'll go and see her.

He hangs up his jacket in the entrance hall, where we can see it.

Wife What about you, you had a good day?

Man 1 Very good. Thanks. Lot of work. And you . . .

Wife I was with her.

He reaches out to her affectionately.

Man 1 And have you heard from him? Did he . . .?

3

Wife He phoned several times, but she didn't want to speak to him.

Man 1 That's to be expected. She's hurt.

Wife You would be.

Man 1 Yes. Did you buy the flowers?

Wife No. They just arrived. They're for you. There's a note.

Man 1 Ah.

He looks at it.

Wife I'm glad you're here. You'll know how to comfort her. You'll find the right words. I don't know what else to say. I'm so angry with him. How could he have done that to her?

Man 1 refers to the note which has come with the flowers.

Man 1 They're from the wife of a patient I operated on last month. This man's been having pain in his leg for years. He had difficulty walking. Now he's all right. Look. 'You changed our lives.' That's nice, isn't it?

He notices that his Wife is elsewhere, preoccupied.

Don't worry. Everything will go back to normal.

Wife You think so?

Man 1 Of course. Don't be upset.

The Daughter appears.

Daughter Why are you saying that?

Man 1 Darling.

Daughter Everything will not go back to normal, Dad. It's too late.

Man 1 No, it's not. Come here. Come and let me give you a hug.

4

Daughter I'm sorry to turn up like this. I feel ridiculous.

Man 1 There's no reason to. You know very well this is your home as well.

Daughter I'm so ashamed.

Man 1 Don't be.

Daughter When you're so busy . . . With your speech to prepare . . .

Man 1 That's all right. Now, what happened? Tell me.

Daughter It's horribly banal.

Wife She was searching through his things.

Daughter His jacket. And I wasn't searching, he'd just left it lying about. I came across a letter in one of his pockets. And I discovered there'd been this girl . . . For months.

Man 1 Do you know her? I mean, do you . . .

Daughter No.

Man 1 And what did he say?

Daughter First of all he denied it. Obviously. Then, when I showed him the letter, he got confused and then he started crying . . . He looked so ugly when he was crying. I was so disappointed with him. Then I left. I told him I didn't want to see him again. That it was all over.

Man 1 But what got into him? This isn't like him, this story. Are you sure you're right? I mean . . . Are you . . . ?

Daughter I've been such a fool. For months, do you understand? For months they've been seeing each other behind my back. And I trusted him. I'd never have believed he could . . . And he was lying to me. Every day he was lying to me. We were trying for a baby.

Man 1 Do you want me to speak to him?

5

Daughter No. Absolutely not.

Man 1 So what are you planning to do?

Daughter Nothing. There's nothing to do. It's all over.

Man 1 You don't think you could forgive him? Try to understand? To . . .

Wife Pierre, they were trying to have a baby.

Man 1 I know.

Wife How do you expect her to forgive him?

Man 1 Sometimes you have to learn to forgive. You have to . . . Don't you think? Maybe it's not as serious as you think it is.

Daughter Not as serious? He's been sleeping with her for months, Dad.

Man 1 Yes, I know, all the same . . . Maybe it wasn't very important to him. Maybe it was . . . a . . . You know, a . . . Yes, I mean . . . I . . .

Wife What?

Man 1 Mm?

Wife Maybe it was what?

Man 1 Nothing.

Daughter Anyway, it's always the same story.

Man 1 Don't say that, darling. He was crying, doesn't that prove . . . ? Doesn't it? What you mean to him.

Wife Pierre.

Man 1 What?

Wife He's been sleeping with this girl for months . . .

Man 1 Yes, I gathered that.

Daughter It's disgusting.

Man 1 I know. Come on . . . Don't worry. Everything'll work itself out.

Daughter No.

Man 1 It will. You'll see. Everything'll work itself out. Things always work themselves out in the end. Trust me.

TWO

(S2): Man 2, his Girlfriend. A bed.

Man 2 I'm trying to think what my life was like before I met you . . .

Girlfriend Nothing.

Man 2 How do you know? You weren't there.

Girlfriend Well, I can imagine.

Man 2 My life was like nothing?

Girlfriend Nothing. A joyless existence. Then you met me.

He smiles. The Girlfriend gets out of bed. She's naked. She sets off to look for a cigarette in the far corner of the room.

Man 2 You're so beautiful.

Girlfriend (*pretending she hasn't heard*) Mm?

Pause. He says nothing. He's happy just looking at her.

What did you say?

Pause. He says nothing. He's happy looking at her, amused. She comes back.

You think so?

Man 2 Yes, I think so.

7

She's back with him.

Girlfriend It's because I love the way you make love to me.

Man 2 In spite of my age . . .

Girlfriend Stop. I've never felt as good as this with anyone.
I could spend whole days with you doing nothing else.

Man 2 With no food. And no sleep.

Girlfriend I've never spent the night with you.

Man 2 No.

Girlfriend Don't you miss that?

Man 2 Mm?

Girlfriend Don't you miss that?

Brief pause.

I miss it.

Man 2 Why? There's nothing interesting about going to
sleep. When I see you, sleeping's not what's on my mind.
Frankly.

Girlfriend Sometimes, I wake up in the middle of the night
and you're not there. I feel lonely. I wake up and feel like
making love. If you only knew. I want to make love to you,
but you aren't there.

Man 2 What do you do then?

Girlfriend If you were there, next to me, you'd find out . . .

Man 2 smiles.

Man 2 I'm going to have to go.

Pause.

Girlfriend You know, I was meaning to tell you . . . I talked
to you about . . . That job they were maybe going to offer
me in Berlin . . .

Man 2 Yes?

Girlfriend Well, it's happening, it's been confirmed.

Man 2 Really? That's . . . that's wonderful.

Girlfriend Yes. I have to give them an answer this week.

Man 2 That's . . . Yes. Are you happy, you must be?

Girlfriend You don't seem unhappy.

Man 2 No, no, I'm . . . On the contrary. I was thinking about you.

Girlfriend If I accept, I'll have to go and live in Berlin. What I mean is, I won't be here any more.

Man 2 I know. I'd worked that out.

Girlfriend At least for a few months.

Man 2 Yes.

Girlfriend Is that all you're going to say?

Man 2 What do you want me to say? Obviously I'd prefer it if you stayed. Obviously. But you have to think of yourself. Of yourself, not of me.

Girlfriend Is that true?

Man 2 What?

Girlfriend You'd like me to stay?

Man 2 Yes. But you have to accept. It's . . . It's a great opportunity. It's . . .

Girlfriend If you tell me to stay, I'll stay.

Pause.

Man 2 No, no. You have to go. And so do I. I have to go. I'm very late . . .

Pause. He reaches for his jacket.

9

Girlfriend Can I ask you a question?

Man 2 says nothing.

Do you and your wife still make love?

Man 2 What's the connection?

Girlfriend I'm asking.

Man 2 Why?

Girlfriend I'd like to know.

Man 2 I can't see the point. Of knowing.

Girlfriend I'm jealous.

Man 2 Stop it . . .

Girlfriend You think that's stupid?

Man 2 Yes.

Girlfriend I imagine you doing it and I feel jealous of her.

Man 2 You've no reason to be jealous.

Pause.

Yes, sometimes we make love. Obviously. But it's . . . it's different. It's a habit, it has nothing to do with . . . This is something else. Why are you asking me this question?

Girlfriend I'd like you to be exclusive to me.

Man 2 Stop it.

Girlfriend What?

Man 2 (*gently*) Stop it.

Pause.

You know I adore you.

THREE

(S3): Man 1, the Young Man. An office.

Man 1 Thanks for coming. It's good of you to come.

Pause. He fetches out two glasses and a bottle.

Obviously, this has to stay between us. It's just between you and me. I didn't tell her I was seeing you.

Pause.

You'll be speaking in complete confidence.

He offers a glass. Pause.

I'd like to sort this thing out, you with me? Insofar as it's possible to . . .

Young Man How? She won't speak to me.

Man 1 That'll pass. But first, I'd like to understand. This story . . .

Young Man What can I tell you?

Man 1 The truth.

Young Man It's so humiliating.

Man 1 For her or for you?

Pause.

You know, I'm not sitting in judgement. We all have our weaknesses. We all have our . . . let's say our demons. But you have to understand, this concerns my daughter. I suffer on her behalf. Her pain is my pain.

Young Man I know.

Man 1 That's why I'd like you to explain it to me. Don't be afraid.

Pause.

I don't want to interfere in things that don't concern me.
I respect you and I wouldn't like to . . . How shall I put it?
Intrude. But you're not speaking to each other. I'm trying to
help you.

Young Man I know.

Man 1 Things were going well between you, weren't they?
I mean . . .

Young Man With Sara? Not all that well.

Man 1 Oh, they weren't?

Young Man She was often aggressive to me. No. Things
were quite tense. Basically, I think she resents me. She's
always resented me.

Man 1 Why?

Young Man For not being like you. She admires you so
much . . . Everyone admires you . . . It's . . . It's not easy for
me to . . . rise to that level. She despised me. Because I
wasn't always able to . . . And I had financial problems . . .
She . . . Whereas this girl . . .

Man 1 Yes?

Young Man She was gentle. It gave me back my confidence.
It made me . . . It's as simple as that.

Man 1 What does she do?

Young Man She's a singer.

Pause.

Man 1 But what are you planning to do now? I mean, this
girl . . . Are you going to go on seeing her? I want an honest
answer. Believe me, I'm not going to judge you. I'd like to be
able to help my daughter avoid unnecessary suffering: you
understand me? That's my only motive: the least possible
suffering for the people I love. Just tell me the truth . . .

Change of tone.

Young Man Do you tell the truth?

Man 1 Excuse me?

Young Man Maybe it never happens to you?

Man 1 What?

Young Man To hide it.

Man 1 What are you . . . ?

Young Man Dream on. You saying it never happens to *you*? Telling a lie.

FOUR

(S2): The Girlfriend, alone.

She's sitting on the edge of the bed. She picks up the telephone. She's weeping. The way she's breathing implies panic.

Girlfriend Hello? Yes, it's me. I know, I know. I'm sorry but I . . . Why aren't you answering my texts? I know. But I need to see you. This evening. Yes. This evening. I have to speak to you. No, listen to me . . . I need to . . . get out of it. It's important, Pierre. I'm not in a good way, not at all. I . . . If you don't come, I . . . I could do . . . I could do something stupid. I could . . . I'm not feeling at all well. Yes. All right. I'll wait for you. I'm waiting for you . . . Hurry . . .

FIVE

(S1): Man 1, his Wife, his two Friends. The living room. There are still flowers there.

Male Friend No, I must tell you, I thought your speech was incredible.

Man 1 You're exaggerating.

Male Friend No, not at all. Ask Delphine, that's exactly what I said to her. Didn't I? It was brilliant. Very intelligent. In a word: incredible.

Wife He wasn't happy with it.

Male Friend He's never happy with anything he does. But I know everybody admired it. Everybody. You saw the reaction? And the applause.

Female Friend And the minister. He admired it very much. He told Delaume.

Wife Yes, he phoned us.

Female Friend Delaume?

Wife No, the minister. He even sent us some flowers . . .

Male Friend Congratulations.

The phone rings. The Wife gets up.

Wife Excuse me a minute.

Male Friend No, I must say I was very proud of you. I mean, obviously I haven't read the report, but it seems your recommendations are . . . I mean, they'll be followed.

Man 1 Let's hope so. No point otherwise.

Wife Hello?

Male Friend Only thing that surprised me was . . .

Wife Hello?

Male Friend How shall I put this? That you openly support Krawzensky's conclusions.

The Wife hangs up and returns to the group.

Man 1 Why not? They seem sound to me.

Wife Sorry. Wrong number. I don't know what's going on at the moment. We keep getting calls like that.

Female Friend Really?

Wife Yes. I can't understand it. Always the same thing. As soon as I answer, they hang up.

Male Friend I thought he was your worst enemy . . .

Man 1 Who?

Male Friend Krawzensky.

Man 1 No . . . It's true our analyses have often diverged, but I've never considered him an enemy.

Wife Yes, you have . . .

Man 1 No, I promise you. Never.

Male Friend You used to say he was under the thumb of the pharmaceutical industry, only interested in money and that . . .

Man 1 Yes, yes, I know what I said.

Male Friend So?

Man 1 So this time his conclusions seemed to me reliable. I thought it right to single him out in my report.

Male Friend A few months ago you were saying the opposite.

Man 1 Well, I've changed my mind.

Male Friend I'm sure there'll be some very positive consequences for the labs that support him . . .

Pause. Slight unease.

Female Friend And your daughter? How is she?

Wife Not so good.

Female Friend Oh, poor thing . . .

Wife Yes.

Female Friend They seemed so close.

Man 1 They were.

Wife They were trying for a baby.

Female Friend What a waste . . .

Wife (*looking at her husband*) Yes. It's sad. There are men who waste the happiness they have in their hand. Sad and strange at the same time. As if they were trying to destroy, destroy and destroy again . . .

Man 1 Would you like another glass?

Male Friend I would, thanks.

Female Friend Jean.

Male Friend What?

Female Friend You're driving.

Male Friend Yes, so I am. Just a drop, then.

> *Man 1 pours a drink for his friend, then pours himself a large glass, which he drinks down in one gulp, much to the surprise of his guests.*

SIX

(*S2*): *Man 2, his Girlfriend.*

The Girlfriend is weeping. She goes to open the door.

Man 2 What's going on?

Girlfriend Thanks for coming. I had to see you. I had to speak to you.

16

Man 2 I don't want you to phone my house. Do you understand? Not like that. Have you considered how risky that is? Lucky it was me that picked up. I . . .

Girlfriend You'd turned off your mobile. And I had to speak to you.

Man 2 That's not a reason. I had guests this evening . . . I don't want . . . You just mustn't do that . . . All right. What's the matter with you?

Girlfriend I ran into your wife just now.

Man 2 What?

Girlfriend I was in . . . And she . . .

Man 2 What are you talking about?

Girlfriend Just now, I ran into her.

Man 2 My wife? Where? And when?

Girlfriend Just now. At the shop. She came in to buy a . . . Don't laugh. She bought a sweater. Your size. She bought you a sweater in the shop. Red. To begin with, I didn't know. I didn't know it was her. So I spoke to her. We even had a joke. I thought she was beautiful. I liked her. And then she gave me, to pay, she gave me her credit card, and I saw her name, I saw your name and I understood. I understood she was your wife.

Man 2 Is that all?

Girlfriend How do you mean?

Man 2 She paid, and then?

Girlfriend Then nothing. She left.

Man 2 So why are you in this state?

Girlfriend I don't know. It's just completely . . . You see, that's not the way I imagined her.

Man 2 My wife?

Girlfriend Yes. For me, she was like an abstraction. An idea. A vague idea. And I imagined her very . . . Very different. I thought she was beautiful and I didn't like that.

Man 2 I don't understand your reaction.

Girlfriend It's as if our situation became clear to me for the first time. This may seem stupid, but . . . That's how it is. All of a sudden, the whole thing became unbearable.

Man 2 What are you talking about?

Girlfriend I want things to change.

Man 2 I understand. But, Sophie, calm down.

Girlfriend Ultimately, this is humiliating for me.

Man 2 Ssh . . .

Girlfriend It's humiliating. Do you understand? I can't do it any more.

He puts his arms round her to calm her down.

Man 2 It's all right now. Calm down. Mm? Calm down, sweetheart.

Girlfriend I want you to tell her the truth.

Man 2 Sorry?

Girlfriend Your wife. I want you to tell her . . .

Man 2 What?

Girlfriend The truth.

Man 2 But why? I mean, what good would it do?

Girlfriend I want to clarify the situation.

Man 2 Clarify the situation?

Girlfriend Yes.

Man 2 But for what reason? The situation is very clear.

Girlfriend You think so? I find it . . . opaque. I can't see anything. I'm in the dark. For example . . . What about us?

Man 2 Us, what us?

Girlfriend What am I to expect from all this?

Man 2 I've already told you. *Nothing.*

Girlfriend You realise what you're saying?

Man 2 I do realise and it's painful for me, but that's the way it is.

Girlfriend We've been seeing each other for over a year, you tell me you love me, and now you're telling me quite coldly that I can expect nothing from you.

Man 2 I've been married for twenty-five years, Sophie. That's the situation. You knew this when you met me. You knew I had nothing to offer you but moments. Moments like the ones we've shared . . . I'm sorry. I can't offer you anything else.

Girlfriend Is that what your love is? Is that it?

Pause. He lowers his eyes.

What am I supposed to do? Wait? Not see you any more? Mm? Tell me, what am I supposed to do?

Man 2 I don't know.

Girlfriend I hate you.

She might do something violent.

SEVEN

(S3): Man 1, the Man in Black. A different office.

Man in Black I'm listening . . . Do you always tell the truth?

Pause.

You see, I'd like to understand what's happened. I think that's a reasonable aspiration. And I can't see what's going to prevent me finding out what *really* happened. What about you, can you see anything that might prevent me from finding out the truth?

Pause.

The truth always appears to those who seek it. There's no exception to that rule. Given time, people will talk. Under pressure, tongues loosen. And we have time. All the time in the world. And we know how to apply pressure.

Pause.

So I'm going to ask you again, very calmly. One last time. And this time, I'm expecting you to answer . . . *What happened?*

Pause.

I'm not sitting in judgement, you understand. I know everyone has their . . . weaknesses.

Pause. The Man in Black laughs.

Not saying anything? Seems to me you've been known to be more talkative. You make speeches . . . Don't you? Perhaps someone helps you to write them? Do people suggest ideas to you? No? Or maybe people blackmail you for favours?

Pause.

Come on, don't be difficult . . . Answer the questions nicely before things start getting complicated for you. *What happened?*

Pause.

Very good. You don't want to say anything. In that case, I'd like to introduce you to someone. (*He picks up a telephone.*) Send him in.

Pause.

Man 1 What are you doing?

Man in Black He's a friend. A mutual friend. I think you'll be happy to see him again.

Man 2 comes in. He's handcuffed behind his back. Man 1 is terrified to see him, as if he's come out of a nightmare. He gets up from his chair. Dread and demoralisation.

Man 1 No, no, no . . . Not him. Please. Not him! I'll tell you everything. Please . . . I'll explain everything to you.

EIGHT

(*S2*): *The Girlfriend.*

The Girlfriend is stretched out on the floor, as if dead. Someone's knocking on the door. Several knocks. She doesn't move. There's a voice from the other side of the door: 'Anybody there? Anybody there? Are you all right? Is anybody there?' Then, silence.

(S1): Man 1, his Wife. After dinner.

Wife I thought they'd never leave. Didn't you? It's not that they're boring, they're nice, but in the end I wanted them to go. Didn't you? We need to talk about this holiday business. I'm thinking maybe they're not wrong. Mm? What do you think about Morocco?

Pause.

Are you all right?

Man 1 Mm?

Wife Is everything all right?

Man 1 Fine, darling.

Wife Doesn't look like it.

Man 1 No. Everything's fine.

Wife You seemed . . . somewhere else.

Man 1 Me?

Wife Yes. During dinner.

Man 1 No, no. I don't think so. You . . . A bit pensive, perhaps.

Wife You don't have any particular problems?

Man 1 No, no. None at all.

Wife Good. Are you operating tomorrow?

Man 1 Mm? No. But I have to spend the day at the clinic. I've got very behind with . . . Because of the commission and this report.

Wife But that's all behind you now.

Man 1 Yes.

Wife And it went well. Everybody said so. Everybody admires you . . .

Man 1 Well, you know, I don't care what people say . . .

Wife When you were making your speech, I can tell you one thing, speaking personally, I was proud of you. I was proud that you're my husband.

Man 1 That's nice. You . . . Are you going to bed?

Wife Yes. Aren't you coming?

Man 1 Mm? Yes. Maybe I'll stay down here a minute. Answer some emails. I won't be long.

Wife You sure you're all right?

Man 1 Yes, nothing to worry about, darling. Everything's fine. Just a few emails I need to answer.

His Wife comes over and strokes his hair tenderly.

Wife Don't be too long. I'll be waiting for you.

She goes out. He stays in the living room on his own, looking sombre and preoccupied. While he thinks, a light gradually comes up on S2, revealing once again the image of the woman on the floor. This time, Man 2 is beside her, as if he's just committed a crime. Blackout.

Act Two

ONE

(*S1*): *Man 1, his Wife.*

Like a slightly distorted version of the start of the previous act.

Wife Ah, there you are.

Man 1 Yes. I've only just finished.

He takes off his coat. He kisses his wife.

Wife Did you get my message?

Man 1 Yes, of course. Is she still here?

Wife No, she's left.

Man 1 Oh? Is she all right?

Wife She's been crying all evening.

Man 1 Poor little thing.

Wife Yes. She was bound to end up the victim. What about you, you had a good day?

He hangs up his jacket.

Man 1 Very good. Thanks. Lot of work. And you . . .

Wife I'm all right.

He reaches out to her affectionately.

Man 1 So what's happened?

Wife I don't really know. She didn't want to go into details. But I got the impression . . .

Man 1 That?

Wife I got the impression he's seeing someone else.

Man 1 Yes, that's what you said. Is that all you know?

Wife She was searching through his things and . . .

Man 1 Why is she searching through his things?

Wife I don't know. That's not the problem.

Man 1 Of course it's the problem! It's just stupid. You don't search through other people's things.

Wife It may be stupid, but if he hadn't done anything wrong, she wouldn't have found anything.

Man 1 There's always something to be found! Always. Often insignificant things. From which you can construct . . . This is ridiculous.

Wife Why are you getting annoyed?

Man 1 I'm not getting annoyed. I'm just saying she shouldn't be surprised if . . . Well. Let's hope this isn't going to be too serious. Did you buy the flowers?

Wife Mm? No, they just arrived.

Man 1 Ah.

He moves past the flowers without looking for a note.

Wife You seem on edge, Pierre.

Man 1 Me? No, I'm sorry. It's just . . . It's this speech I have to write for tomorrow. So, yes, I am a bit tense. Sorry.

Wife I understand. It's important.

Man 1 Yes, the stakes are . . . Some people can put terrible pressures on you and . . . Anyway, I have to think carefully about what I'm going to say.

Wife You'll do it very well. You always do.

Pause.

Man 1 Maybe I should call her. I . . . Am I supposed to know about this?

Wife Yes. I told her I'd told you.

Man 1 What do you think? Should I call her? I don't want to be too intrusive . . .

Wife You're her father.

Man 1 Precisely.

Pause.

Wife They were trying for a baby.

Man 1 Sorry?

Wife That's what she told me just now.

Man 1 Poor thing. But everything'll work itself out.

Wife You think so?

Man 1 Of course. You don't leave someone because of some minor infidelity. That would be absurd.

Wife You're wrong. She doesn't want to speak to him again. She left the flat telling him it was all over. She never wants to see him again.

Man 1 She said that because she's angry, but . . .

Wife No, I'm telling you. She never wants to hear another word about him. It isn't going to work itself out.

Man 1 Don't you think so?

Wife I know her. There are certain subjects on which she's . . . She gets that from me. She'll never forgive him for having lied to her. Never.

Slight unease.

TWO

(S3): The Man in Black, Man 2. The office.

The Man in Black is alone in the office. He picks up the telephone.

Man in Black Send him in.

The door opens. The opening of the door is an event in itself, dream-like.

Man 2 appears. He's in handcuffs – and the scene is like a repeat of what we've already seen – except that Man 1 is not in the room.

Come in. Come in, I said. Don't be afraid. I'm not going to eat you . . .

Man 2 hesitates – which amuses the Man in Black – and finally comes over to him.

Sit down.

Man 2 sits down. The Man in Black consults a file, which no doubt contains previous statements by the man facing him.

After a while, he finally decides to look at him.

There's a prince who goes out hunting with his huntsmen.

Man 2 Sorry?

Man in Black I'm telling you a story. If that's all right by you. Apparently you've no objection to telling stories yourself. Am I right?

Brief pause.

There's a prince who goes out hunting in the depths of the forest. Hours pass, but he encounters no game. Nothing. Then suddenly he sees a majestic stag escaping across a clearing. A large white stag, like something stepping straight out of a dream, and the prince is entranced by this apparition. He starts to follow it and rashly strays away from his huntsmen. He crosses the clearing and catches sight of it again, in the distance, but the stag vanishes almost at once. And the prince plunges deeper into the forest. Of course, he has heard tell of hunters who have never returned and the most sinister rumours flying around concerning this forest. But at this moment, entranced as he is, and perhaps because he believes himself more cunning than the others, he can't help himself and he plunges into the forest. He catches sight of it again, several times. But every time, it vanishes almost at once. Stubbornly, the prince continues to follow it. Until the moment it dawns on him that the animal has disappeared for good. That maybe it never existed. That night has fallen . . . And that he is completely lost . . .

Brief pause.

Am I boring you? You don't seem to be concentrating very hard. Or perhaps you don't enjoy this kind of story?

Man 2 shrugs.

I don't either, tell you the truth.

He throws the file in the waste-paper basket.

I prefer to stick to the facts. Don't you? I'm sure you agree. That's why I suggest that we go through everything again from the beginning. Idea is to clear up all the confusion . . . Would you like that? Marvellous. So . . . Tell me . . . And this time I want the truth. *What happened?*

THREE

(S2): Man 1, the Girlfriend. A bed.

Man 1 I'm trying to think what my life was like before I met you.

Girlfriend Nothing.

Man 1 How do you know? You weren't there.

Girlfriend Well, I can imagine.

Man 1 What do you imagine?

Girlfriend *(playfully)* I imagine you were . . . A dreadfully sad man, passionate about your work and your success and your routines . . . And about power . . . And you landed on me . . .

Man 1 Miraculously . . .

Girlfriend Yes. And there was a great transformation and now you're finally interested in interesting things . . .

Man 1 Such as?

Girlfriend Such as . . . Me. Am I right? Before you met me, weren't you quite a sinister piece of work?

The Girlfriend gets out of bed, laughing. She's naked. She sets off to look for a cigarette in the far corner of the room.

Man 1 You're so beautiful.

Girlfriend *(pretending she hasn't heard)* Mm?

Pause. He says nothing. He's happy looking at her, amused. She comes back.

You think so?

Man 1 Yes, I think so.

She's back with him.

Girlfriend It's because I love the way you make love to me.

Man 1 In spite of my age . . .

Girlfriend Stop. I've never felt as good as this with anyone. I could spend whole days with you doing nothing else.

He smiles at her. He quickly checks his watch. There's a sense that he's going to have to leave.

You remember when we first met, you used to call me 'my beloved'? I liked that. I thought that was pretty. Very promising . . .

Man 1 But you're still my beloved.

Girlfriend You've stopped saying it.

Man 1 Have I?

Girlfriend Yes.

Pause. Suddenly she seems gloomy.

Man 1 What's wrong with you?

Girlfriend Me?

Man 1 Yes. You're not like you usually are.

Girlfriend You're right . . . I don't know what to expect from all this. Sometimes I'm scared of getting old. Of waiting for you to no purpose. And of finding myself . . . With nothing.

He checks his watch.

You have to go?

Man 1 Yes. I've a meeting at the clinic.

Girlfriend Are you operating today?

Man 1 No. Just consultations.

Girlfriend You have a beautiful thumb.

She puts it in her mouth and sucks it.

Man 1 I have to go.

Girlfriend You once told me you had a special insurance policy just for your thumb . . . Is that true?

Man 1 All surgeons do. In case there's an accident . . . It's a surgical instrument.

She's continuing to suck it provocatively and erotically, making him smile.

What are you doing?

Suddenly she bites it. He pulls his hand away sharply.

Ow! What's got into you? You can't do that. You've hurt me.

Girlfriend And you've hurt me.

Man 1 You bit me.

Girlfriend I'm hungry.

Man 1 It's not funny, Sophie. You've hurt me.

Girlfriend Oh, I'm sorry . . . Anyway, you're insured.

Man 1 Not funny.

Pause.

Girlfriend Will you come and see me on Friday? On my birthday . . .

Man 1 I can't. I already told you.

Girlfriend Dinner with your wife, is that it?

Man 1 Please . . .

Girlfriend She has all the luck.

Man 1 Sophie . . . What's your problem? What's wrong with you today?

Girlfriend I'd like you to be exclusive to me.

Man 1 Stop it.

Girlfriend What?

Man 1 (*gently*) Stop it.

Pause.

You know . . .

Girlfriend What do I know?

Man 1 You know it isn't possible.

Pause.

Girlfriend Can I ask you a question?

Brief pause.

The clinic belongs to your wife's family, doesn't it? If that wasn't the case, if you weren't afraid of losing everything, would you leave her for me?

FOUR

(*S1*): *The Wife.*

The telephone rings. The Wife appears. She picks up.

Wife Hello?

Pause.

Who's there? Hello? Hello? Who's there? Who are you? Who's there?

They've hung up. Pause. She hangs up and freezes as she sees Man 1's jacket, hanging in the entrance hall. She's tempted to search through the pockets . . .

FIVE

(S3): Man 1, his Male Friend. An office.

Man 1 I hope I'm not disturbing you.

Male Friend Of course not. Are you kidding? What's the matter?

Man 1 Yes, I wanted to talk to you. That's why I've come by.

Male Friend I'm all ears.

Man 1 You see, you're my only friend. And I have to . . . I absolutely have to talk to somebody.

His Friend goes over to close the door, which was ajar.

Male Friend Is there a problem?

Man 1 Yes, I think so. But it's delicate.

Male Friend Tell me. Maybe I can help you.

Pause.

Man 1 But this has to stay between us.

Male Friend Of course.

Man 1 It's delicate because it concerns Laurence.

Pause.

I've . . . Let's say I've definitely made a mistake . . . A few months ago . . . I . . . Well, I've no right to complain about this, but . . . I met someone.

Male Friend Oh?

Man 1 Yes. A girl . . . And I got fond of her . . . Well, you know the kind of thing I mean . . .

Male Friend Yes, yes.

33

Man 1 To begin with, I went a bit crazy. She's young, she's beautiful, she likes making love . . . she brought me back to life, if you know what I mean. But now it's become difficult to manage. A real nightmare. She . . . she's a bit unstable. Yes. I didn't realise it until today. And she . . . How can I put this? She's threatening to tell Laurence everything.

Male Friend Shit. Why?

Man 1 I don't know. I never promised her anything. She's always known my situation. I've never lied to her . . . But I'm telling you, she's not very balanced . . . Obviously she's started imagining things. About us living together . . .

Male Friend And what are you planning to do?

Man 1 I don't know, I'm lost.

Male Friend I can see that.

Man 1 I've never been as lost as this. I don't even know who I am any more.

Male Friend And you think she'd be capable of telling? I mean . . .

Man 1 nods.

Ah.

Man 1 That's why I'm so terribly afraid . . .

Male Friend In that case, perhaps you ought to tell Laurence the truth. Straight out.

Man 1 I can't. Obviously it would be a relief for me. But she'd be destroyed. Believe me, it would destroy her.

Male Friend Maybe you have no choice.

Man 1 No, I couldn't do that . . .

Male Friend What else can you do? If she has to find out, far better to do it through you. Don't you think?

Man 1 It's horrible. I feel as if my life is collapsing. Just think, this girl phones the house . . . There are these continual anonymous calls . . . She could tell her everything at any given moment. I don't know what to do.

Male Friend I'm telling you. You have to tell Laurence everything.

Man 1 Never. I'm never going to do that.

Male Friend If she loves you, she'll forgive you.

Man 1 She won't.

Male Friend She will . . . After all, it's not as if you're a criminal. She'll be angry with you, of course she will. Yes. But in the end she'll forgive you. Don't you think?

Brief pause.

Don't you think?

Man 1 No.

SIX

(S2): Man 2, the Girlfriend.

The Girlfriend is on the floor, as if dead. There's blood. It's the continuation of an image we saw earlier. Man 2 goes over to sit on the bed. Pause. He looks at her. Then he dials a number on his mobile.

Man 2 Right. It's done.

He hangs up.

SEVEN

(S1): Man 1, his Wife, the Man in Black (in place of his Male Friend), the Female Friend. The living room (there are more and more flowers).

Man in Black No, I must tell you, I thought your speech was incredible.

Man 1 You're exaggerating.

Man in Black No, not at all. Ask Delphine, that's exactly what I said to her. Didn't I? It was brilliant. Very intelligent. In a word: incredible.

Wife He wasn't happy with it.

Man in Black He's never happy with anything he does. But I know everybody admired it. Everybody. You saw the reaction? And the applause.

Female Friend And the minister. He admired it very much. He told Delaume.

Wife Yes, he phoned us.

Female Friend Delaume?

Wife No, the minister.

Man in Black Congratulations.

The phone rings. The Wife gets up. So does Man 1, like a jack-in-the-box.

Man 1 Leave it. I'll get it. If you'll excuse me a minute.

Man in Black No, I must say I was very proud of him. I mean, obviously I haven't read the report, but it seems his recommendations are . . . I mean, they'll be followed.

Wife Apparently, they're thinking of asking him to be President of the Science Council . . . But that's still confidential.

Man 1 Hello?

Man in Black Wonderful. No, the only thing that surprised me was . . .

Man 1 Hello?

Man in Black How shall I put this? That he openly supports Krawzensky's conclusions.

Man 1 hangs up and returns to the group.

Man 1 Sorry.

Wife Who was it?

Man 1 Wrong number.

Wife I don't know what's going on at the moment. We keep getting calls like that.

Female Friend Really?

Wife Yes. I can't understand it. Always the same thing.

Man in Black I thought he was your worst enemy . . .

Man 1 Sorry?

Man in Black I thought he was your worst enemy.

Man 1 Who?

Man in Black Krawzensky.

Man 1 Oh. No . . . I . . . Our analyses . . . But I've never considered him . . .

Wife Yes, you have . . .

Man 1 No, I haven't. Never!

Man in Black You used to say he was under the thumb of the pharmaceutical industry, only interested in money and that . . .

Man 1 (*inscrutably*) Yes, yes, I know what I said.

Man in Black So?

Man 1 So this time his conclusions seemed to me . . .
I thought it right to single him out in my report.

Man in Black A few months ago you were saying the
opposite.

Man 1 (*fiercely*) Well, I've changed my mind!

Man in Black Why are you getting annoyed?

Man 1 Because you're making unpleasant insinuations.

Man in Black Really? What are they? All I'm saying is that
there'll be some very positive consequences for the labs that
support him . . . There's a lot of money involved.

Pause. Unease.

Female Friend What are you doing for the holidays?

Wife Oh, don't talk to me about it, we've got nothing
planned. It's always like this, coming up to Christmas.
People book so far in advance, there's nothing available any
more. I wanted to go somewhere sunny, but at the last
minute . . .

Female Friend Yes, no vacancies.

Wife None. What about you, are you . . . ?

Female Friend We go to Morocco every year. It's the best
place in December. We take a room in a riad. The weather's
mild. It's very relaxing. That's what you ought to do.

Wife Yes, that's a good idea. Maybe. What do you think?
We're not at all good at holidays. Pierre is always working.
At one time, when the children were small . . . But, now . . .

Man 1 Would you like another glass?

*He refills his friend's glass. Suddenly, the Girlfriend
appears. She's covered in blood. A moment of suspension.*

Man 1 knocks the glass over. Everyone stands up. Pause. Like a suspension of reality.

Girlfriend What have you done? What have you done?

Man 1 Nothing.

Wife But . . . Pierre . . .

Girlfriend Why have you done this?

Man 1 is seized by panic.

Man 1 But I haven't done anything . . . I haven't done anything.

Girlfriend Do you realise what you've done?

Man 1 But I haven't done anything . . . It wasn't me.

Wife Pierre?

Man 1 It wasn't me. It was . . . I swear it wasn't me!

Blackout.

EIGHT

(S3): The Male Friend, Man 2. In the Friend's office.

Male Friend So where do you meet?

Man 2 Her place. She has a bedsit, quite central.

Male Friend Every day?

Man 2 No, from time to time. But often enough.

Male Friend Has this been going on long?

Man 2 More than a year.

Male Friend Oh, well . . .

Man 2 Yes.

Male Friend What kind of a relationship is it? I mean, is it romantic or just . . . ?

Man 2 I don't know any more. At the beginning, I suppose . . . yes, we loved one another. Then she began to frighten me. And I distanced myself from her a bit.

Male Friend Why didn't you stop seeing her at that point?

Man 2 I was afraid. I was afraid she'd be angry with me and . . .

Male Friend You were afraid of revenge?

Man 2 Yes, certainly. Something like that. I was waiting for her to meet someone else, to leave me of her own accord . . .

Male Friend But that never happened.

Man 2 No. And now I don't know what to do. The other night she called the house. I don't even know how she got hold of my landline. I had guests for dinner. Luckily, it was me who picked up. She was crying. She was in a complete state. She'd bombarded me with texts all evening. She wanted me to come and see her that night. She wanted to talk to me. It couldn't wait. I said it wasn't possible, I wasn't alone, but she threatened me. She told me if I didn't come and see her that night, she'd turn up at my house, never mind my guests, and she'd tell the whole truth.

Male Friend So what did you do?

Man 2 I made up an excuse. And I went to see her. She was crying. We fought. It was horrible.

Male Friend You can't go on like this.

Man 2 No. But I don't know what to do. My life is a constant misery. A constant misery, I assure you.

Male Friend I can imagine.

Man 2 I can't sleep. I can't concentrate any more. All I can think about is this little disaster hanging over my head.

Male Friend So why don't you talk to her? The girl, I mean . . .

Man 2 She doesn't want to listen. I've told her I don't love her any more. She doesn't believe me.

Male Friend What about your wife?

Man 2 What about my wife?

Pause.

I would never want to hurt her, my wife. I love her, do you understand?

Pause.

Male Friend There is one thing we could do.

Man 2 What?

The Friend picks up the telephone.

Male Friend Send him in.

Man 2 is watching him, uncomprehending.

He's a friend. He'll be able to help you.

Man 2 Really? . . . Are you sure?

Male Friend Trust me.

A door opens.

NINE, PART I

(S2): *Man 1, his Girlfriend.*

Girlfriend Why are you looking at me like that?

Man 1 Like what?

Girlfriend You look furious.

Man 1 You know me too well.

Girlfriend All this time . . .

Pause.

What? Tell me.

Man 1 There were these calls last night . . .

Girlfriend What calls?

Man 1 Stop it!

Pause.

You know very well. Anonymous calls. To the house.

Girlfriend So? What does that have to do with me?

Man 1 I want to know if it's you.

Girlfriend You think it's me making these calls?

Man 1 Isn't it?

Girlfriend Why would I want to call your house?

Man 1 Tell me if it's you.

Girlfriend You scared I'll speak to your wife? Is that it?

Man 1 Listen, I don't know what you're playing at, but this can't go on.

Girlfriend No, it can't go on.

Man 1 Tell me the truth.

Girlfriend You talk to me about truth? When you're lying to everyone. Do you know how long you've kept me waiting? You . . .

Man 1 Don't let's start on that again.

Girlfriend You promised me . . .

Man 1 What? What did I promise you?

Girlfriend You've never made me any promises?

Man 1 No. Never. Never!

Girlfriend You're a real piece of shit.

Man 1 Stop.

Girlfriend A piece of shit.

Man 1 Listen, we have to . . .

Girlfriend I'm going crazy.

Man 1 . . . try to stay calm.

Girlfriend I can't. I can't. Because of you, I'm going crazy!

Man 1 But what do you want?

Girlfriend You're asking me that?

Pause. She might do something violent.

I've given you everything. Everything. I even turned down going to work in Berlin for your sake.

Man 1 That was your decision.

Girlfriend No, you told me not to go.

Man 1 I never said that.

Girlfriend You asked me not to go. So I stayed. I work in a crappy shop. I . . . I sell sweaters to your wife. I'm on my own. I sleep on my own. No one looks after me. I . . .

Man 1 What is it you want, Sophie?

Girlfriend I want you to tell your wife the truth.

Man 1 That's impossible.

Girlfriend We can't go on like this.

Man 1 I'm telling you, it's impossible.

Girlfriend Then I'll tell her. I'll tell her the truth.

Man 1 Sorry?

Girlfriend If you haven't the courage to do it, I'll do it myself. We can't ruin our relationship just because you haven't the courage . . . no, that'd be too absurd.

Man 1 You will not say anything to my wife.

Girlfriend You'll thank me for it, one day.

Man 1 Why are you doing this? What have I done to you? I've always been . . . We've spent some beautiful moments together. We've . . . both of us. And is this what it's come to? You threatening me?

Girlfriend Because you're incapable of keeping your promises.

Man 1 I never promised you I'd . . .

Girlfriend Stop lying. Stop this constant lying!

Man 1 But I'm not lying. Listen . . . I don't know what it is you're looking for . . . And stop drinking.

He takes the glass out of her hand.

Girlfriend Hit me. Go on!

Man 1 Stop it.

Girlfriend I know you're dying to. So go on. Hit me! Hit me!

Man 1 Please stop it. You're pushing me over the edge.

Girlfriend I'm the one who's over the edge!

He buries his face in his hands.

Man 1 (*beaten down*) We have to talk. You need to understand my position. If you speak to my wife, you'll destroy her. Do you realise that? There are certain bonds between us . . . After all these years . . . You can't just turn up and lay all that to waste. You can't do that to me. Not to me.

Girlfriend Talk to your wife. Afterwards, you'll see, we'll be happy again. Talk to her, or I'm going to have to talk to her.

44

(*S1*): *The Wife, the Daughter*

Wife Tell me.

Daughter What do you want me to say?

Wife I don't know. Talk to me. How are you?

The Daughter shrugs.

Have you seen him?

Daughter Did you know he'd been to see Dad? He turned up at the clinic and they talked to each other . . . Did you know that was happening? He can't stop himself. He can't help interfering in other people's business.

Wife He was trying to help you.

Daughter There's no point. I don't want to see him any more. Surely it's easy to understand! He's disappointed me so badly. What's worse is, after we broke up, our friends started to tell me stories about him . . . things they didn't dare tell me before . . . and it seems I was the only one who didn't know . . . And I realised this girl wasn't the only one . . . That . . . How could I have been so stupid? In the end, it's always the same story. Always! You think you've met someone different. You tell yourself: 'At least, he's not like all the others.' But when it comes to it, all men are the same.

Wife Don't say that . . .

Daughter It's true. As if none of them, not *one*, ever escaped that iron law, that miserable little iron law. If you knew how much I loathe them . . . What's going on in their heads? What is this compulsion to use us like this? To abuse us? To see us as *prey*?

The Wife gets up and moves off a little way.

You know what, I'm going to end up living with a woman. It'd be much more interesting. Much less . . . I'm serious, I hate them all.

She realises her mother has moved away.

What? What is it?

Wife Nothing.

Daughter Did I say something?

Wife Mm? No, no.

Pause.

Daughter Mum? What's the matter?

Blackout.

TEN

(*S3*): *Man 1, the Man in Black. An office.*

Man in Black I'm listening.

Man 1 I had a dream last night . . .

Man in Black Go on.

Man 1 There was this girl . . . She'd come to lay my life to waste.

Pause.

I needed some advice. I knew I was in a, what, complicated situation.

Man in Black Yes . . .

Man 1 This girl . . . She was very . . . Totally out of control. She was threatening me. I didn't know what to do. I was lost. I've never been so lost . . . I was like a child, left abandoned in a forest . . . A deep forest. I was sweating. I was afraid. But I couldn't manage to wake up. It was a hideous dream, a dream you couldn't escape from. Like a prison. Without bars. Without a door. Impenetrable.

Man in Black Go on.

Man 1 I . . . I went up flights of stairs, I knew these stairs led to a room and that it was the girl's room. Her room.

Lights slowly go up on S2.

When I reached the landing, I knocked on the door. I knocked several times. She was supposed to be in, so I was worried. Because there was no answer. I knocked again. I said: 'Anybody there? Anybody there? Are you all right? Is there anybody there?' But there was no answer. Nothing. I was worried. So I pushed at the door. It wasn't locked. I simply pushed at the door . . .

Pause.

Man in Black *And what happened?*

Pause.

Come on, don't be difficult. Answer the questions nicely before things start getting complicated for you. *What happened?*

Pause.

Very good. You don't want to say anything. In that case, I'd like to introduce you to someone.

He picks up the telephone.

Man 1 No, wait . . .

Pause.

(*He's breaking down.*) The door was open. There was no sound. I went in. I just went in. To check that everything was all right. That's all. And I found her. Stretched out. On the floor. She'd fired a bullet into her chest. She'd killed herself. My beloved. That's what happened. She'd killed herself. Because of me. My beloved. Because of me . . .

ELEVEN

(S2): The Girlfriend, Man 2.

This sequence has begun upstage, simultaneous with Man 1's narration: it illustrates what's being said: Man 2 comes into the room and discovers the Girlfriend stretched out on the floor, as if dead. No blackout.

TWELVE

(S1): Man 2, the Wife. After dinner.

The Wife speaks to Man 2 as if he were in front of her, whereas the sofa is empty. All three sets are lit: Man 2 is still beside the Girlfriend, who is on the floor.

Wife I thought they'd never leave. Didn't you? It's not that they're boring, they're nice, but in the end I wanted them to go. Didn't you? I know you, I could see you were bored. Weren't you? I had that feeling all the way through dinner. The feeling you were somewhere else. It was as if you'd gone missing. I don't know. You don't have any particular problems, do you? Tell me, Pierre . . . Are you all right? Is everything all right, darling?

Man in Black *(S3)* What about your wife? Does she suspect anything?

Wife In any case, that was quite a good idea of theirs, Morocco. Do us good to go somewhere, don't you think? Now that you're going to have a bit of spare time. We

could . . . It'd make me happy. We could maybe go
somewhere. Couldn't we? What do you think? Mm? Pierre?
What do you think? Pierre?

*Suddenly panicky, she looks across towards S2 and then
towards S3, as if she were trying to grasp something
which is escaping her.*

Pierre?

Act Three

ONE

*(S1): Man 2, the Wife, the Girlfriend. The living room.
More and more flowers.*

*Like an even more distorted version of the start of the
previous act.*

Wife Ah, there you are.

Man 2 Yes. I've only just finished.

He takes off his coat. He kisses his wife.

Wife You didn't get my message?

Man 2 No. What about?

Wife About Sara. She cancelled dinner.

Man 2 Oh? Why?

Wife She didn't really tell me, but my sense was, well, that
she'd had a row with Arthur.

Man 2 Nothing serious?

Wife I don't think so. She asked me to apologise to you.

Man 2 Shame. I was looking forward to seeing them. What
about you, are you all right?

Wife I'm all right.

He hangs up his jacket.

Man 2 So what shall we do? You want to go to a
restaurant?

Wife Just as you like . . . But everything's ready.

Man 2 Then let's eat here. The two of us.

He reaches out to her affectionately.

Wife While I think of it, there was a call for you.

She goes to look for the piece of paper on which she's written the message. He sees the flowers.

Man 2 More flowers?

Wife Yes. Everybody's sending you flowers. Here we are, look . . .

She's found the piece of paper.

Seems rather important. Some policeman.

Man 2 What?

Wife Superintendant Messard. He wanted to speak to you. Apparently. I asked him what it was about, but he didn't want to tell me.

Man 2 Oh?

Wife He told me it was important. And that you needed to ring him back. Tomorrow if possible.

Man 2 Okay, fine.

Wife I wrote down his number for you.

He puts the piece of paper with Messard's number in the pocket of the jacket he's just hung in the entrance hall.

Any idea what it's about?

Man 2 Mm? No. I'll see. This often happens. Some sort of routine enquiry or . . . Maybe . . . I don't know. But nothing to worry about.

Wife There isn't a problem?

Man 2 Of course not . . .

Wife Seemed quite important.

Man 2 Don't worry. Everything will go back to normal.

The Girlfriend appears, just like the Daughter in Act One.

Girlfriend Why are you saying that?

Man 2 What are you . . . ?

Girlfriend Everything will not go back to normal. It's too late.

Wife Pierre? Are you all right?

Clearly, the Wife can't see the Girlfriend, who's appearing to Man 2 like a ghost. It's as if he's mesmerised by her.

Man 2 Mm? Yes, yes. Everything's fine. I . . . I'm just a bit . . . tired. I . . .

Wife Do you want to eat something?

Man 2 Yes. Why not? But what would you prefer? You . . . You wouldn't rather go to a restaurant? The two of us?

Wife Just as you like. If you're tired, we can eat here. Everything's ready.

The Girlfriend sits down on the sofa, as if nothing's happened.

Man 2 No, maybe I'd rather . . . I'd rather . . . what would you like best?

Wife Let's stay and have dinner here. That'd be simpler.

Man 2 All right.

Wife Unless you'd prefer to go out . . . But, look, everything's already prepared for Sara . . .

Man 2 Yes, fine. Let's do that. You're right.

Wife Good. All right. I'll go and fix it.

She goes out. Man 2 turns towards the Girlfriend. Pause.

Girlfriend It's horribly banal. They were searching through my things.

Man 2 What?

Girlfriend They'll obviously have to search the place. And they'll come across . . . I don't know. Some trail that will bring them back to you. That's why that policeman came here. They're after you, Pierre. There'll be something that'll do you in. Your texts, for example. You really think I erased them?

Man 2 You told me you . . .

Girlfriend I kept them all. Every one. That counts as proof, don't you think? What did you expect? That you'd be able to get away with what you did? Why should you get away with it? Because you're a man? Because you're rich? Because you have powerful friends? No one escapes the consequences of his actions. No one, you hear me? It's just a question of time now. So get ready to pay. Because that's the way it's going to end, this story. You're going to pay. You're going to pay for what you've done.

TWO

(S3): Man 1, his Male Friend. In the Friend's office.

Man 1 I can't sleep. I can't concentrate any more. All I can think about is this little disaster hanging over my head.

Male Friend What about your wife?

Man 1 What about my wife?

Pause.

I would never want to hurt her, my wife. I love her, do you understand?

Pause.

53

Male Friend There is one thing we could do.

Man 1 What?

The Friend picks up the telephone.

Male Friend Send him in. He's a friend. He'll be able to help you.

The Young Man comes in.

I've explained your situation to him.

Man 1 But this is . . .

Male Friend Don't worry. He's a friend. He won't say anything. But he thinks he can help you.

Man 1 How?

Young Man (*speaking a foreign language*) Нам надо эту девушку заставить молчать.

Man 1 What? What did he say?

Male Friend He said we have to stop this girl talking.

Young Man И в таком случае есть только один верный способ.

Man 1 I don't understand.

Male Friend You understand very well.

Pause.

Young Man (*with a very strong accent*) There is only one way to stop someone from talking.

Man 1 But we can't. We can't do something like that.

Male Friend What about her? She's about to destroy your life. Do you let her do something like that? All you're doing is trying to save your life. That's all.

Man 1 I don't know.

Young Man Я знаю одного человека, которые может оказать такую услугу. Но конечно, этому есть цена.

Male Friend He knows someone who can do you this favour. Obviously, there's a price.

Man 1 What price?

Young Man (*strong accent*) A favour.

Man 1 I don't understand.

Young Man (*strong accent*) My friend. He is also friend of Krawzensky. Does this name mean something to you? If you give him the favour he is asking you, I think he can arrange that she will say nothing.

Male Friend Now do you understand?

Man 1 But you can't . . .

Male Friend From each according to his ability.

Man 1 It's not possible.

Young Man (*strong accent*) Everything will happen very simply. You won't even hear about it. You won't be responsible. It'll be our secret. No one else will know about it. And everything will go back to normal.

THREE

(*S2*): *Man 2, the Girlfriend.*

On the floor, the Girlfriend lies, as if dead. Man 2 wipes the fingerprints from a pistol and puts the gun in the Girlfriend's hand. Then he goes over to the bed. Pause. He dials a number on his mobile.

Man 2 Right. It's done.

He hangs up.

FOUR

(S3): The Man in Black, Man 1. The office could be a psychoanalyst's consulting room.

Man 1 So last night I had a dream. I was wearing a mask, a white mask, expressionless, but nobody seemed to have noticed. I gave my speech, and I realised that no one knew I was wearing a mask, no one seemed to be aware I was crying behind my mask. Finally, at the end of my speech, everyone applauded. They kept saying: 'What an extraordinary man! What an extraordinary man!' Then I wanted to take off the mask. In front of everybody. That'd surprise them, I said to myself. I put my hands up to my face and tried to take it off, the mask, but there was nothing to take off, nothing, and I understood that what I'd first thought of as a mask was actually my real face, and that I no longer had an expression or any tears or any feeling – nothing.

Pause.

I think that was the moment I decided to kill her. Not to kill her myself, obviously. I'm . . . incapable of doing anything like that. But I'd been told about someone who . . . Who could do this kind of job for me. My only condition was . . . Not to know anything about it. Not a single detail. I was just to get a telephone call. I was told there'd be a voice, the voice of the man who . . . And all it would say to me was: 'Right. It's done.' Nothing else. And then, everything would go back to normal. I would never hear this story referred to again. Never. And my life would pick up just as before.

Brief pause.

That's all.

Man in Black That's all? Really?

Pause.

Does the name Krawzensky mean anything to you?

Pause. No answer.

No? Really? Krawzensky? I'm amazed.

Pause.

And? Then what happened?

Man 1 Then? I woke up. My dream was over.

The Man in Black writes something in his notebook. No blackout.

FIVE

(S1): The Wife, the Male Friend, the Female Friend. Man 1 and the Man in Black are still in the office (S3). Man 1 is simultaneously in the room with them and somewhere else. There's someone else in S1, a dream figure: a Woman with a stag's head.

Male Friend I thought he was your worst enemy . . .

Man 1 *(from S3)* Sorry?

Male Friend I thought he was your worst enemy.

Man 1 *(from S3)* Who?

Male Friend Krawzensky.

Man 1 *(from S3)* Oh. No . . . I . . . Our analyses . . . But I've never considered him . . .

Man in Black *(from S3)* What?

Male Friend You used to say he was under the thumb of the pharmaceutical industry, only interested in money and totally corrupt . . .

Man 1 *(from S3)* Yes, yes, I know what I said.

Man in Black (*from S3*) So?

Man 1 (*from S3*) So this time his conclusions seemed to me . . . I thought it right to single him out in my report.

Man in Black (*from S3*) A few months ago you were saying the opposite.

Male Friend Let's hope for your sake the Science Council doesn't find out about this. I'm not sure they'd appreciate it.

Female Friend Definitely not. It could have some very awkward consquences . . .

Man 1 doesn't look very well.

Wife Is everything all right? Are you all right, Pierre?

Man 1 (*from S3*) Yes, yes. Everything's fine. Just a . . . Everything's fine, thanks.

Wife Would you like a glass of water?

Man 1 (*from S3*) No. No, thanks.

She gets up to go and fetch him a glass of water.

Man in Black (*from S3*) Are you feeling all right?

Man 1 (*from S3*) Sorry, I'm really sorry . . . I . . . I've had a lot of work recently.

Male Friend Don't worry.

The Wife comes back with a glass of water.

Wife Here, take this glass of water.

He doesn't.

Man 1 (*from S3*) Thanks. Thanks, darling. But it'll pass. It was just . . . I was just feeling a bit sick.

Pause.

Male Friend You ought to take a holiday. Now you've finished your report . . .

Man 1 (*from S3*) Yes, certainly.

Wife Pierre never takes holidays.

Male Friend You ought to.

Female Friend You should do what we do. Have a week in Morocco.

Male Friend It would do you good. Both of you.

Man 1 (*from S3*) Yes, yes. Good idea.

The doorbell rings. Man 1 (in S3) looks at his watch.

Male Friend Are you expecting someone?

Wife No. I . . . I don't think so.

The Wife hesitates, surprised as well. Who could be at the door at this time of night? She looks for some clue in her husband's eyes.

Man 1 (*to the Man in Black, continuing the account of his dream*) So she went to answer the bell. But there was no one there. Just a bouquet of flowers left in front of the door . . .

She opens the door. She finds the bouquet of flowers.

Wife What's this? Someone's delivered this . . . A bouquet of flowers. More flowers. Our house looks like the Botanical Gardens. Who can it be this time . . .?

She reads the card.

Ha . . .!

Female Friend What?

Wife Look at this, Pierre . . . They've written . . . 'Sincerest condolences' . . . What . . . There must be some mistake. Don't you think? There's no name . . .

Female Friend Show me.

The Wife shows her the card.

Weird.

Wife They must have mixed it up with someone else's, or . . . I don't know. Why would somebody send this to us? I mean, to us? . . . They must have made a mistake. Pierre? They must have made a mistake . . . Pierre? What does this mean?

Man 1 has gone pale. Gradually, lights come up in S2 and we discover the Girlfriend, sitting on the bed. She's brushing her hair.

Man 1 *(from S3)* The police called. I went in to see them the next day. They asked me questions. I didn't dare ask them how they'd got to me. They asked me if I knew you, how I met you . . . They were trying to understand what had happened. I told them the truth.

Wife *(from S1)* Pierre?

Man 1 *(from S3)* Then they asked me if to my knowledge you might have any reason to put an end to yourself, if you'd ever talked to me about . . . And I told them. I said you'd been unhappy recently. I said you'd been unhappy because of me. The one asking me the questions looked at me understandingly. He knew we were . . . that we'd been lovers. I imagine he'd read the texts. He said that would be all for today. And they never called me back. Never.

Brief pause. Unease in the living room . . .

Female Friend Jean . . .

Male Friend Yes, perhaps we ought to be going . . .

Female Friend Yes, I think so, I think the time has come . . . Early start tomorrow and . . . Thanks again for everything. It was delicious. It's always a pleasure to . . . I mean, we've spent a wonderful evening with you.

Male Friend Yes, wonderful.

Female Friend Come on . . . Speak soon. Take care.

The two Friends leave the room. The Wife remains, on her own, bewildered. She's still holding the card. The Woman with the stag's head is still there.

Man 1 *(from S3)* You must be terribly angry with me.

Girlfriend *(from S2)* Ssh.

Man 1 *(from S3)* I can't sleep any more. My life has become an endless nightmare. Scenes play over and over again in my head. Repeat themselves obsessively. I . . . I can't concentrate any more. I've taken a few days off from the clinic . . . I can't operate any more. I . . . I've never felt so lost . . .

Girlfriend *(from S2)* Ssh . . . come on, calm down.

Man 1 *(from S3)* Sometimes I want to tell my wife everything.

Girlfriend *(from S2)* Tell her what?

Man 1 *(from S3)* Everything that's happened.

Girlfriend *(from S2)* How would that help you?

Man 1 *(from S3)* I might be able to sleep again.

Girlfriend *(from S2)* Wouldn't do you any good.

Man 1 *(from S3)* I want to pay for what I've done, you understand me? I want to find a way to pay.

Girlfriend *(from S2)* Don't talk such rubbish. You've nothing to reproach yourself for. It was just, I couldn't wait any longer. One day, I preferred to leave. Simple as that. I was offered that job in Berlin . . . You remember? I'd always dreamed of being a singer. Since I was a little girl . . . I called them and the job was still open. So I left. I had to disappear, one way or another. Do you see? Today, it's to a cabaret in Berlin, another day, it'd be somewhere else . . .

One day, you'll come across me again, maybe on stage in London or Paris . . . Who knows? In the meantime, all you have to do is tell yourself I'm still here. Somewhere, far away, and that I'm still singing.

Man 1 (*from S3*) My beloved. My beloved.

S2 goes back into darkness, as does S3. The Wife is alone in the living room. Pause. Blackout.

SIX

(*S1*): *The Wife. Even more flowers.*

Lights up almost immediately. The Woman with the stag's head is no longer there and the set suddenly seems more realistic.

We hear the voice of Man 1, as if he's seeing out his guests.

Man 1 Right. Very good . . . Safe journey . . . Thanks very much. Yes, see you soon . . .

Man 1 returns.

Wife Is that it?

Man 1 That's it. At last . . .

Wife Stop it. They're nice . . .

He shrugs.

Man 1 I thought they were never going to leave.

Wife Yes, I could see you were finding it a bit of a slog. You were somewhere else . . .

Man 1 Me?

Wife Yes. During dinner. You weren't with us. You were . . . Am I wrong?

Man 1 No, no. I don't think so. You . . . A bit pensive, perhaps. But . . .

Wife You don't have any particular problems?

Man 1 No.

Wife Are you sure?

Man 1 Yes. Why?

Wife Sometimes, I have the feeling . . . you're hiding things from me.

Man 1 What are you talking about?

Wife What I say.

Pause.

You can talk to me, you know . . .

Man 1 Yes, I know. But I . . .

Wife You've changed. For quite a while now. I feel it. As if there was something tormenting you . . .

Pause. Man 1's desire to confess becomes almost palpable.

Why won't you tell me what's happening to you?

Pause.

Mm?

Man 1 is looking at her. Does she know something? Does she suspect something? Might he really be able to confide in her?

I'm on your side, you know that.

She takes his hand as she speaks to encourage him to confide. This simple gesture seems to astonish and distress Man 1. She becomes aware of this.

What's the matter?

Man 1 I'm so lucky to have you.

She smiles affectionately at him.

Wife Don't change the subject.

Man 1 There is no subject. I have no particular problems. I promise you. It's just, these last few weeks have been really testing.

Wife I know.

Man 1 I'm just tired, that's all. Some people can put terrible pressures on you and . . . Yes, the stakes are . . . I've had to take some difficult decisions . . . But it's all over now. I probably need . . . That's why . . . I'm thinking about what they were saying. We never take a holiday. Maybe we should . . . Shall we? Go to Morocco. Or somewhere else. Get some sun. What do you think?

Wife Yes, that'd be good.

Man 1 Just the two of us. How long has it been since we were just the two of us?

Wife A long time.

Man 1 Too long.

Wife Yes.

She smiles at him. He takes her in his arms. And kisses her on the forehead.

Man 1 I love you, you know that.

Brief pause.

Wife Shall we go to bed?

Man 1 If you like. I just have a few emails to write, then I'll join you.

Wife Now?

Man 1 Won't take long.

Wife All right. I'll go and get ready. I'll be waiting for you.

She smiles tenderly at him but she doesn't leave. She looks at him for a long time.

Man 1 What?

Pause.

What is it?

She indicates 'nothing' with her head. But her serious expression seems to suggest the opposite. An apparently interminable pause, loaded with subtext.

Then she leaves. He's alone in the room.

In the distance, a young woman's voice singing a song.

Light gradually comes up on S2, while he's thinking, and again there's the image of the woman dead on the floor. Except this time it's the corpse of a freshly killed stag that's lying on the floor.

Another light comes up on S3, and Man 2 appears, seated on the couch: he's wearing an expressionless white mask. And a red sweater. The Man in Black sits facing him, looking at him.

Then the Man in Black slowly begins to take off his make-up.

Suddenly, almost silently, Man 1 begins to weep.

Then the lights go down and only Man 1's face remains lit, a white light, stronger and stronger, as if it were burning into this face.

Blackout.